A Puzzle for S

Story by Annette Smith

Photography by Lindsay Edwards

"Look, Scruffy," said Josh.

"Here is a puzzle for you."

Scruffy looked at

the seesaw,

and the box,

and the blocks.

"Come to the seesaw, Scruffy,"

said Josh.

Scruffy ran into the box.

"No, Scruffy!" said Josh.

"Come here.

Come to the seesaw!"

Scruffy went up the seesaw.

And he went down the seesaw.

"Good dog, Scruffy!" said Josh.

"Run into the box, Scruffy,"

said Josh.

Scruffy ran to the blocks.

"No, Scruffy!" said Josh.

"Run into the box!"

Scruffy ran into the box.

"Good dog, Scruffy,"

said Josh.

"Can you go over the blocks?"

Scruffy went over the blocks.

"You are good at the puzzle,

Scruffy," said Josh.